FROM ARMY TO MULTI MILLIONS IN REAL ESTATE

From Army to MULTI Millions in Real Estate

THE BLUEPRINT

Clavacia Love

Love Estates Property Management LLC.

Copyright © 2023 by Clavacia Love & Love Estates Property Management LLC.

All rights reserved. No part of this book may be reproduced in any manner whatsoever without written permission except in the case of brief quotations embodied in critical articles and reviews.

Love Estates Property Management LLC., 2023

Contents

1	Table of Contents	2
2	Purpose, why do this?	4
3	Uncle Sam's Twenty-year Retirement	8
4	Owning VS Leasing	11
5	Power of Credit	14
6	Loans	18
7	VA Specialty Loans	22
8	Short-Term VS Long-Term Tenants	26
9	Network	35
10	Knowing your demographic and market areas	37
11	Long-term VS Short term cash-returns	41
12	Where do tenants come from?	44
13	REFI to free-up VA home loan	46
14	What's not seen, or told in real estate?	48
15	Closing	62
16	Resources	64

17 References 65

From Army to MULTI-MILLIONS in Real Estate
By: Clavacia Love

Author has been featured in these
networks as other familiar televised
networks

1

Table of Contents

Table of Contents
Purpose, why do this?
Uncle Sam's Twenty-year Retirement
Owning VS Leasing
Power of Credit
Loans
VA Specialty Loans
How the VA IRRRL Works
Benefits of Using the VA IRRRL to Scale a Real Estate Portfolio
How Many Times Can an Individual Use the VA IRRRL?
Eligibility Requirements:
Short-Term VS Long-Term Tenants
Network
Knowing your demographic and market areas
Long-term VS Short term cash-returns
Where do tenants come from?
REFI to free-up VA home loan
What's not seen, or told in real estate?

Realtors
PMI/ DOWNPAYMENT
Pros of PMI
Cons of PMI
BUYING DOWN INTEREST RATES
Points
Refinance
Adjustable-Rate Mortgages
Government Programs
PROPERTY MANAGEMENT
CONTRACTORS
DO NOT GET SCAMMED
Closing
Resources
Home searching sites
Helpful Sources
References
About the Author
One Last Thing!

2

Purpose, why do this?

My name is Clavacia Love Smith, and my story began when I was a young child in elementary school. I grew up in a split home as my parents were still very young their selves being only 15 years older than me. My mother and father were both separated, and I would spend half the time with each side of my family. One side of my family all had jobs and immediately started working and the other side had been entrepreneurs primarily in the field of real estate. My parents had given me the book "Rich Dad Poor Dad for kids" by Robert kiyasoki and told me I had to read it. Having me to read it again, again, and again. At one point, I felt as though I had known the entire book without even having to open the page from cover-to-cover and I felt like at the time a lot of it had went over my head being so young, but as I grew older it began making more sense. I had been able to place myself in the book and understand it from the perspective of the book's protagonist, and then apply it to my own personal life as well. Being older now, I can see the differences between having a job and opposed to working for yourself and being self-employed as an entrepreneur.

There are both PRO's and CON's to being employed as well as being an entrepreneur (please see table below)

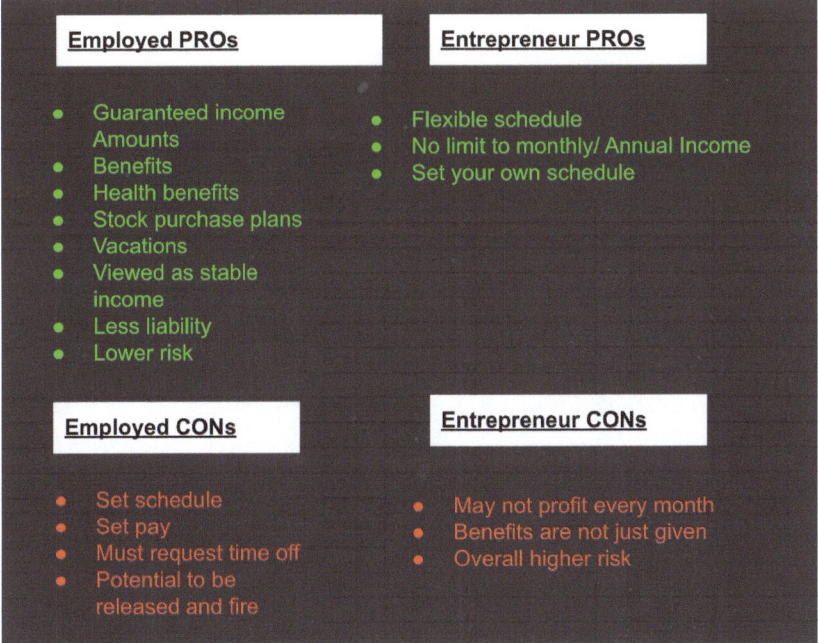

I started asking myself why I heard the different complaints and types of struggles that I had been hearing between the different sides of my family. I had seen and made the decision at that point that I wanted to be more like the entrepreneur side and assume those different risks and stride for the different rewards I seen affiliated with it, opposed to the life of set guaranteed income. As I wanted to play football and look into a HBCU my mother had severe health issues when I was 16 years old and I had decided to turn down the football scholarships I had been offered out of state and stay local for college. The colleges that accepted me did not offer me any football opportunities, but I chose to stay local so I could support my family as needed. Being a full-time college student, I did not have the money needed to live for myself let alone my siblings, and that pushed me to join the military. I enlisted in the Army and thought that it would be more beneficial for me to study ROTC in college and get promoted to a higher rank than what I had started at initially. Being in ROTC allowed for me to receive additional stipends and benefits. Knowing at this point I would pursue an entrepreneur route in REI (real estate investments) I decided to get a loan that USAA offered to college students graduating from ROTC for a loan at $25,000 with no interest or payments until after college.

This book is ideally for a person in the military that is looking to find secondary income passively. There are benefits and tools in this book that can be utilized by those that are non-military, however, given my background and experience I wanted to highlight those from similar walks of life that also served. This book will assist in giving the blueprint that was able to work for me and allow for me to elevate into a higher tax bracket and receive income, while still being able to pursue my dreams on a day-to-day basis at my leisure. Being in the military we all have seen those people that would do a full 20 years and retire and still have to work, however, what if they invested in real estate at the start of their careers and utilized the income from their tenants to pay off the homes? This would mean that as they are transitioning out of the military, they would be able to not only receive military compensation monthly, but also rental income monthly! Allowing them to not have to look for additional funds from employment, because they would be self-employed and if work with managing seems to be too tedious, they can budget for a property management. Even if the soldier is to purchase a home near a military installation that they PCS to and never plan on returning to that is not a problem, because all soldiers and veterans know that when someone is leaving to a new duty station that the Army is sending a replacement immediately after and that someone will need to rent or occupy their home. Over the next couple of chapters in this book you will find some of my strategies and insights on the real estate industry and how it can be beneficial to someone both entering or exiting the military that is looking to grow their income.

3

Uncle Sam's Twenty-year Retirement

This chapter talks about life after a military career. We all have heard the stories from our beloved recruiters about all the perks and benefits of joining the military and making so much money, traveling the world, and after 20 fantastic years of work retiring with a nice picket fenced home. However, this is typically not the case of what happens. Research conducted here shows the percentage of veterans that retire from the military and still need to find employment after they separate.

According to a survey conducted by Blue Star Families in 2019, 37% of military spouse respondents reported that their family's income was not enough to meet their basic needs (Blue Star Families, 2019). This data shows that even with the retirement benefits, some veterans and their families still struggle to make ends meet. Additionally, a study by the National Veteran Education Success Tracker (NVEST) found that 41% of veterans reported working full-time, and 8% reported working part-time, while also attending school

(NVEST, 2021). This data suggests that a significant percentage of veterans who retire from the military still need to find employment in order to sustain ordinary living.

Challenges Faced by Veterans in Finding Employment

Veterans face several challenges when it comes to finding employment, including the lack of civilian work experience, a limited professional network, and mental health issues. For example, according to the Military Times, one of the biggest obstacles that veterans face in finding employment is the lack of a clear career path and job training (Military Times, 2021). Moreover, veterans often face difficulty in translating their military skills into civilian skills that employers can understand. We have to realize that the branches of the military from Army to Marines, or Navy to Air Force have big differences that are not always common knowledge let alone the thought of a civilian employer with no prior military background understanding and comprehending the skills that we have and how they are relevant.

Another challenge that veterans face is the limited professional network, which can make it harder for them to find job opportunities. According to a report by the Institute for Veterans and Military Families, veterans often have a smaller professional network than their civilian counterparts, which can limit their job opportunities (Institute for Veterans and Military Families, 2020). If we travel the world from state to state, and in most cases different countries we are not given the opportunity as most Americans to find stable connections that are going to make us successful in finding the career path that relates to our two decades of training and get our foot in the door above an entry level salary.

Finally, many veterans also suffer from mental health issues, such as post-traumatic stress disorder (PTSD) and traumatic brain injury (TBI), which can make it harder for them to find and maintain employment. According to a study by the Substance Abuse and Mental Health Services Administration (SAMHSA), 18.5% of veterans returning from Iraq or Afghanistan reported symptoms of PTSD or depression (SAMHSA, 2019). These mental health issues can lead to difficulties in adjusting to civilian life and finding employment. The question to ask is do any of us after adjusting to each permanent duty station want to actually find another job in the first place. Most of us would have left our family and friends for most of the day if we are working within the states, or for a year or more if we are prepping to deploy and go overseas once we include the demobilization process. Truthfully, it is not fair in the slightest to have to endeavour being separated from our loved ones even more than we have already been deprived.

In conclusion, while the unemployment rate for veterans who served on active duty in the U.S. Armed Forces after September 2001 has decreased, there is still a significant percentage of veterans who retire from the military and still need to find employment in order to sustain ordinary living. These veterans face several challenges, including the lack of civilian work experience, a limited professional network, and mental health issues. To address these challenges, it is crucial to provide more job training and education programs for veterans, as well as support for mental health services. By providing more resources and support, we can help veterans transition into civilian life and find meaningful employment.

4

Owning VS Leasing

Owning a home versus leasing is a topic of debate when it comes to housing options. While leasing offers more flexibility, owning a home has several financial gains that can prove to be advantageous in the long term. This section will explore the financial benefits of owning a home versus leasing, with research studies conducted regarding the subject.

One of the primary financial benefits of owning a home is building equity. Equity is the difference between the market value of a property and the amount owed on the mortgage. As homeowners pay off their mortgages over time, they build equity, which can later be used for various purposes, such as funding retirement or purchasing another property, funding a wedding, traveling, or any other expenses that one might find relative. According to a report by the National Association of Realtors, homeownership builds wealth over time, with the median net worth of a homeowner being 80% higher than that of a renter (NAR, 2020).

In addition to building equity, homeownership provides several tax benefits that leasing does not. Homeowners can deduct mortgage interest and property tax payments from their federal income taxes, potentially reducing their tax liability. According to the Tax Policy Center, homeowners can save thousands of dollars in taxes each year by taking advantage of these deductions (Tax Policy Center, 2020).

Owning a home can also provide financial stability and predictability. Unlike leasing, where landlords can increase rent or change lease terms at any time, homeowners have a fixed mortgage payment that remains the same throughout the life of the loan. This predictability can make budgeting and financial planning easier, as homeowners can accurately anticipate their housing expenses over the long-term due to the fact that you are locked into a contract with the bank until the home is paid off in entirety at what you can set to be a fixed rate.

Furthermore, owning a home can provide a hedge against inflation. As inflation rises, the value of money decreases, but the value of real estate tends to increase. As a result, owning a home can be an effective way to protect against inflation and maintain purchasing power over time. You can be creative in several ways that will be discussed in the later chapters of this book on how you can even lower your payments to give yourself consecutive extra funds for the remainder of your home loan.

While leasing offers more flexibility and lower upfront costs, homeownership provides several financial benefits that can have a significant impact on an individual's long-term financial well-being. By building equity, providing tax benefits, offering financial predictability and stability, and providing a hedge against inflation, owning a home can be a wise financial decision.

In conclusion, owning a home versus leasing offers several financial advantages that can have long-term benefits for individuals and their families. From building equity to tax benefits, providing financial stability and predictability, and offering a hedge against inflation, homeownership can be a smart financial investment. As a result, individuals should consider the financial benefits of owning a home when deciding on their housing options.

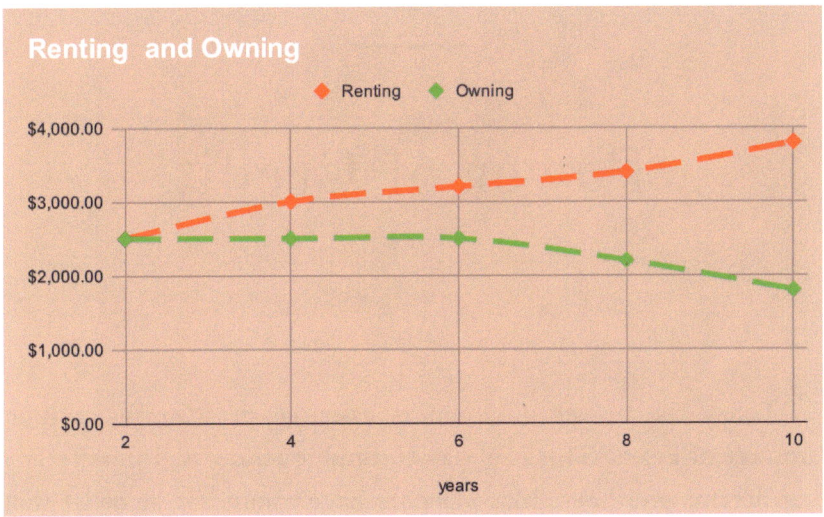

The illustration above is a line-graph depicting how market levels will increase for renters and how a property owner can gradually decrease their monthly payments overtime. Homeowners will steadily increase their rents just as everyone else is to maximize their profits, however, you are locked in to a fixed rate typically with a home loan. In addition to having the fixed mortgage rate you also can have other factors that can contribute to having lower payments such as paying off a majority of the interest as years pass, lowering home insurance, paying extra payments towards a principal balance, or even refinancing into a lower interest rate!

5

Power of Credit

Today the power of credit is essential in acquiring a high amount of assets. This is a way to fund, operate, and finance any big dreams you have. Many people have a mindset or belief that to start a business that they must have the disposable funds within their account to market, supply, and scale their business to the next level. However, this is untrue given the fact that you can use your credit to apply for both loans and credit cards. It will take some research into looking into as different financial institutions will vary as frequently as several times throughout an individual day, but there are different credit card agreements that will offer interest free payments. This means that someone can be approved and funded to make the necessary purchases for their business and not have to pay the money back immediately. If you can buy the necessary utilities, marketing tools, or assets needed to build or grow clientele depending on the business that you have you might be able to start seeing a cash-return. With the money that is acquired from your investment you will be able to start making payments back on the loan or line-of-credit that was initially started prior to any interest accruing. Thus, meaning you can start the business and start making money with little to no money spent. Once the initial expenses or monthly debts are settled, one can begin to see profits. In terms of real estate particularly investors can see different types of profit all at once, however, this will be discussed later throughout this reading the differences between cash-profits and equity.

These loans or lines of credit can be utilized in any manner that seems to make the most sense to include, but not limited to:

- **Additional dwelling Units (ADU)**
- **Renovations**
- **Land Scaping**
- **Initial purchases, refinancing,**
- **Furnishing**
- **Separate adjacent business**

With that in mind, there are different types of loans and credit cards that are available to consider what makes the most sense to you given market fluctuations and personal preferences. Resources on what credit cards and loans are offered at the end of this book through Bankrate.com and they will show you what banks are offering the best rates at any particular time. When you get further down the line and are looking to develop, furnish, or renovate your property you are also able to do this without having to spend actual cash. You can utilize other forms of credit or loans. For example, I was able to utilize the credit cards offered at loans and Home Depot in order to furnish and renovate my rental properties. They offered 0% interest payments on purchases of certain amounts "As long as they are all for one project" meaning as long as they were all purchased together. Keep in mind that ALL OF THIS is business, and therefore it is negotiable to a certain extent. Make sure as you are applying and opening the different credit cards that you are reading the stipulations and fine print as anything and everything is subject to change, and the information that I am giving is based off the time of me currently writing this and my experience over the last year from 2021–2022-time frame. Interest free payments can be allowed for me to obtain a fully furnished home, purchase the necessary materials for renovation, and go live on my first set of Airbnb rentals without any major money out of pocket. The money that was spent out of pocket was the money to pay contractors and inspectors for the property. This can be avoided if you are handy with your hands and able to do the work yourself, some of the work I was able to do myself through the use of social media such as YouTube, Instagram, and Tik Tok. However, some things like moving furniture I needed assistance since I only had a two-door car or carrying it upstairs. If you are looking to save yourself costs in labor of others it might be of interest to look into investing in a utility truck or van, which is possible to write off on your taxes as a business expense (Please consult with your CPA on this first).

The photo above depicts before and after images in which tenants were evicted and trashed the home, alongside the renovations that were made after. Now of course, you will retain their deposit and hopefully required them to have insurance that covers this during their stay. However, you can keep that cash in your account for paying contractors for labor or covering the mortgage during your period of vacancy. Given that the damages in this particular scenario exceeded the deposit and I wanted to rehab the home and get it back rented out as soon as possible, I used credit cards with 0% interest payments to fund the materials needed and cash from deposits to pay for labor and the mortgage.

6

Loans

When you are looking to acquire your first initial investment you are offered the VA Loan, which will guarantee to a financial institution that you are credible and reliable to repay the loan on your home. However, I would NOT recommend utilizing this benefit for your first investment property. I would suggest to first look into different state benefits. Every state has a long list of benefits that can be used to assist its residents with making that initial leap or purchase of a home. Using this first you can purchase up to a four unit dwelling, meaning it can be residence for four separate families at any given time and this would be something I would highly recommend. However, it does not limit you to this purchase and you are allowed to purchase a single-family residence (one unit), a duplex (two unit), a triplex (one unit), a townhouse (one unit), or even a condo (one unit). It is very important to look very closely at the agreements and conduct great levels of due diligence (personal research on the investment). When you are purchasing a home, you are given a due diligence period and this is the timeframe you are allowed to conduct any research that you find necessary on any property you are looking to acquire. This is the timeframe when you typically are allowed to enter and inspect the property, call the city, and see what you are allowed to do with the property, bring anyone from your team (Contractors, landscapers, management, family, business partners, or whoever you see fit) to conduct research and a thorough analysis of the home. This is also the time of which you are allowed time to give a counteroffer based off of your findings. With this you can ask the seller of the property to make adjustments to correct any issues found with the home that you are all able to come together and agree on. Also, most state loans for a first primary home will have guidelines that guarantee the home must be move-in ready meaning that it is safe and does not have to undergo major repairs in order to be liveable. This will protect you and be in your benefit as to requiring the seller to spend funds on repairs that will be required in order to close on the deal.

My suggestion with this being your first investment is to utilize one of these homes as a primary residence first and for example if you were living in a state such as Los Angeles, California where any single unit will be around $400,000 you can utilize this loan and acquire a four-unit apartment. This means that this property will be estimated in value for at least $1.6 million ($400,000 X 4 Units). The catch with this is that you are obligated to utilize this as a primary residence yourself for in most states a minimum of one year and other states or loans this time frame might vary. This does not mean that you are unable to occupy it while you have a roommate covering the portion of rent that you would be receiving from the unit that you are living if your property has multiple bedrooms in all or your particular unit.

The next type of loan that I would like to introduce would be a conventional loan, this would more so be for a property that is not your first purchase and typically would be for investment property and they would require you to have a down-payment that can range from 15-25%, but you are also able to express a few things. One being that your other property is fully occupied and producing additional income for you per your taxes, bank statements, or leasing agreements and that you have had life changes. Some of the life changes can be an increase in family size, new location of your job, or other special circumstances that would require you to have a different living situation in another home. You can then save the money that you were able to receive from passive income monthly living rent free with your tenants and roommate as a down payment of 5% if you express that this will be utilized as a secondary home of residence for yourself (and your family). Whether this is all factual or not, you can utilize this verbiage in order to acquire another property ONLY using a small percentage down that was all acquired from passive income, and yes this also can be another 4-unit property. My recommendation here would be to check in with the bank and see what you are able to get approved for in regard to how much money you have saved up for that 5% down payment and for your purchase. If you believe you are ready and have the funds you can get another piece of property and once again based off Los Angeles, get another property ranging from anywhere being $400,000 and up depending on how many units you are approved and comfortable purchasing. None the less if you follow this strategy your net worth can now grow an instant $2 million off of this strategy and have a total of 5-8 doors (doors being the term used to reference the number of units that you own given the thought that some might be different home types like condos, town homes, single-family, or multi-units).

Now, at this point in time I would look to use the VA home loan. Using the VA home loan can allow for you to acquire another property with no money out of your pocket again. Keeping in mind that there WILL BE closing costs (a compilation of the various fees related to origination of the loan such as taxes, insurances, filing fees, and some other costs that will all be broken down for you in your closing documents). I would highly encourage you to spend money on getting a professional inspector to come out and check on everything in your new home. This is something that can very much vary in costs depending on how large your home is, the level of experience of the inspector, and all the services that they offer. This references back to the section prior in this reading that spoke on having the seller fix the issues that are found in the purchase and saving you costs. Most inspectors will check things that most people are not typically going to notice or have the resources to check on their self-such as the roof, the foundation on the floor, all appliances, and more. I would also like to suggest that you have the home checked for pests and this should include looking for rodents, termites, or any other living creatures that might be occupying or destroying your new investment. This is something that can be at additional cost to you separate from your inspector. However, it is for your safety because you are going to be required to spend money monthly on this home and it is for your business. The costs that are spent on these inspections will be far less than the costs of repairing it after the fact, and thus this would be something that you would want to take the opportunity to seize during your due diligence period. These are recommendations that I would like to highly recommend for all properties you purchase regardless of the loan type, however, with the VA home loan similar to the loan that you are using for your first purchase of the state home loan it is very strict and has a standard/criteria that the home must meet in order for the home to close such as it being livable and up to a particular code.

7

VA Specialty Loans

The VA IRRRL (Interest Rate Reduction Refinance Loan) is a beneficial loan program available to veterans and active-duty service members who have an existing VA loan on their primary residence. The VA IRRRL allows borrowers to refinance their current VA loan to obtain a lower interest rate, which can lead to a reduction in monthly mortgage payments. This, in turn, can provide more cash flow that can be used to invest in real estate and potentially scale a real estate portfolio.

Now, a lot of people are afraid when it comes to using the VA home loan because it will utilize their eligibility and they want to ideally save that entitlement for a forever home. However, research from Leslie Cook in her article with Money.com shows otherwise. Leslie says, "In order to qualify for an IRRRL, your new interest rate must be at least .5% lower than your current rate, for a fixed-rate loan to fixed-rate loan refinance. If you are refinancing a fixed rate mortgage into an adjustable-rate mortgage, the starting rate must be at least 2% lower" meaning you can in fact reutilize these benefits. This is wonderful, given the fact that not only are you able to purchase the home with no down payment for two homes that can depending on your buying power bring you up to a net worth of a million dollars, but you can also purchase multiple homes if you are able to have a better interest rate. There are multiple strategies that can be taken when making a purchase, however, it would always be in your best interest to have the lowest interest rate possible to allow for you to maximize your profits and save as much as possible. Given the regulations stated above you are more so forced to only refinance into a VA IRRRL when the market will save you money on your current assets. She continues to say, "You must wait at least 210 days from the date of the first payment you made on the loan you want to refinance, and you must have made at least six consecutive monthly payments" which simply shows the lenders that you have paid down some of the loan and can also be consistent. This will also assist with showing that you are not looking to work the system and are intending on occupying the home without the need of having additional documentation to prove your case and be accused of any form of mortgage fraud.

How the VA IRRRL Works

The VA IRRRL program is designed to simplify the refinance process for veterans (including those in the national guard/ reservist) and active-duty service members. It does not require a new certificate of eligibility or an appraisal, and borrowers are not required to provide income or employment documentation. The loan is also assumable, which can be beneficial for investors looking to sell a property in the future. This also means that you can assume the loan from other veterans that are selling their home and avoid paying anything down while simultaneously obtaining another asset!

Benefits of Using the VA IRRRL to Scale a Real Estate Portfolio

The primary benefit of using the VA IRRRL to scale a real estate portfolio is the reduction in monthly mortgage payments, which can free up additional cash flow. This cash flow can then be used to invest in additional properties, which can help to diversify an existing portfolio and potentially increase overall returns. In addition to the reduction in monthly mortgage payments, the VA IRRRL can also provide other benefits that can help investors scale their real estate portfolio. For example, the program allows borrowers to switch from an adjustable-rate mortgage (ARM) to a fixed-rate mortgage, which can provide more stability and predictability in monthly payments. This can be especially beneficial for investors who plan to hold onto a property for a longer period of time. Moreover, the VA IRRRL program can help investors to build equity in their existing properties faster. By reducing the interest rate on a mortgage, borrowers can allocate more of their monthly payment towards the principal balance, which can help to pay off the loan faster and build equity in the property.

How Many Times Can an Individual Use the VA IRRRL?

The good news is that there is NO LIMIT to the number of times an individual can use the VA IRRRL program. According to the Department of Veterans Affairs (VA), borrowers can use the program as often as they wish, as long as they meet the eligibility requirements.

Eligibility Requirements:

To be eligible for the VA IRRRL program, borrowers must have an existing VA loan on their primary residence and be current on their mortgage payments. Borrowers must also have a good credit score and a stable source of income to qualify for the loan.

The VA IRRRL can be a useful tool for veterans and active-duty service members who are looking to scale their real estate portfolio. By reducing monthly mortgage payments and providing other benefits such as the ability to switch from an ARM to a fixed-rate mortgage and build equity faster, the VA IRRRL can help investors free up additional cash flow that can be used to invest in additional properties. As with any investment strategy, it is important to carefully evaluate the potential risks and rewards of using the VA IRRRL to scale a real estate portfolio before making any decisions.

8

Short-Term VS Long-Term Tenants

Cash-Returns VS Equity

Now there are multiple ways to see profit in this type of business from cash profits to equity growth. You can see that you might have monthly expenses to give an example of $1,500 to include the mortgage, utilities, and the cost of the furniture. Now let's say your rental on Airbnb/long term tenants is around $2,500 each month. You are able to see that you are able to pay all of your expenses and still have a remaining $1,000 left over. This means that you are seeing a cash return monthly of $1,000. Which is amazing, however, at the same time you are gaining equity at the same time. The Earth is not expanding, however, the population of people on the Earth is growing and this takes us to supply and demand. The supply of real estate or land for purchase is NOT increasing, but everyone needs a place to call home or a place to conduct business, and therefore the demand is steadily increasing each and every year. The renovations that are done in addition to the consistent payments on the loan each month all contribute to the growth of equity. Meaning the money that your tenants are paying each month that your turn-around and send to the mortgage company allows you to have more equity in your property. Swapping out a small ceiling fan and upgrading to something more modern will increase your overall home value. All of this can be assessed in a couple of different ways. Reaching out to a loan officer that specializes in H.E.L.O.C. (Home Equity Line of Credit) and they have two different options that they can typically offer to you. For example, let's say you have $100,000 in equity and different banks offer anywhere from 70-80% of your equity in the loan. Meaning that they will give you anywhere from $70,000 to $80,000 that you can utilize to reinvest in your real estate portfolio, a car, a wedding, a vacation, or into another business that you are very passionate about. Now you will have to pay this back, however, it is typically at a lower interest rate and a great sum of money. This allows you to completely fund or start up your business, and this enables you to jump start a career, get your dream car, or go on your dream vacation you have always wanted and pay smaller amounts than what most would have to pay. This refers to the previous section about obtaining and maintaining a good credit score. They will run your credit and verify income just as a traditional loan, which is nothing different from what you had to do to make the initial purchase of the home.

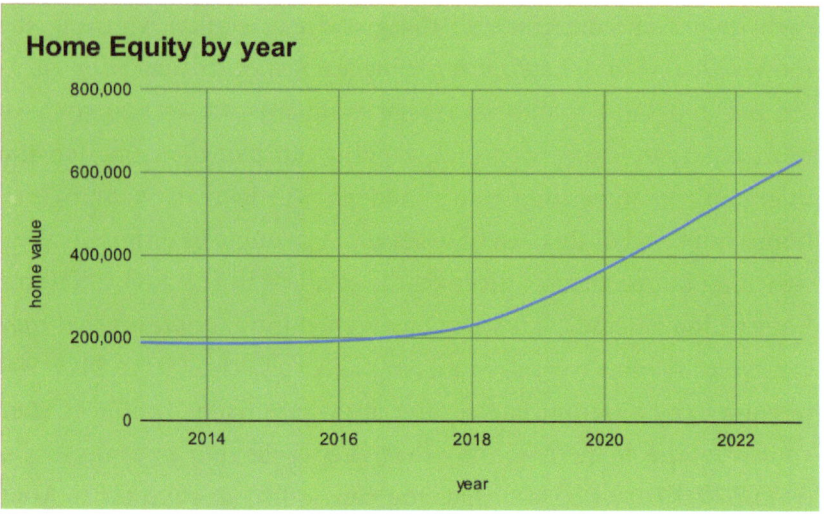

The above photo is a line-chart showing the equity from my first home. I purchased the home in 2021, however, as shown the value has steadily increased. The home was around $200,000 in 2014 and the chart shows every couple of years it has been able to grow in value up to the point where I made my purchase. The key takeaway in the illustration is equity growth that comes with Real Estate just from buying and holding a home.

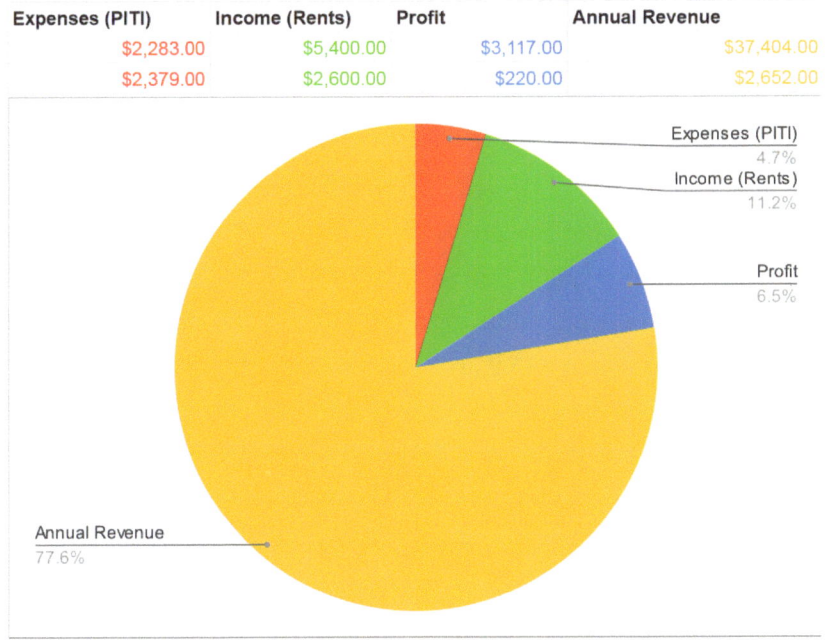

The photo above is a pie-chart breaking down the expenses, income, profit, and annual revenue from my first two properties. This can offer an example of how you can purchase your first couple of properties and receive an immediate cashflow. This example is showing cashflow from a long-term rental. The expenses are compiled of principal interests, taxes, and insurance (PITI). The income (rents) is the fun portion as it pertains to how we see our cash returns on our investments. The rents collected are for the scenarios where we decide to get long-term tenants, however, we also could have income coming in from short-term tenants as well. The profit section is the amount of money left over after subtracting the expenses monthly. Finally, the last section annual revenue is the amount of money you would make at the end of the year (profit x 12 months).

Now there is a lot of different ways to make money off of your new income hassle property. Some ways can be short-term income and others are long-term, and both come with PROs and Cons Typically, doing long term rentals will be favored and are more commonly used across the world, however, the downside is that long-term can come with a ton of headaches and less money. The benefit of this method is you have a less hassle and risk in most cases as long as your tenants are paying you are able to calculate your monthly income. You can subtract the regular expenses and maintenance fees such as the mortgage, accounting for regular wear and tear, or any other unexpected occurrences. Then, you can add the amount that you are charging your tenants each month and budget. Typically, when people stay longer, they get a discount as it is consistent income for the homeowner. This allows for safer planning and budgeting on a month-to-month basis.

When it comes to short-term renting this is a higher risk, but can have far more profits. It can come with far more costs than that of a long-term rental. When it comes to short term rentals in 90% or more cases you will have to have the home fully furnished with furniture and appliances rather than in long-term renting where the typical expectation is to have the house be livable and have appliances such as refrigerators and a stove. This means you have to invest more to add toiletries, utilities, furniture, appliances, decour, and any other features you want to set your place over the top. You also have to account for cleaning fees in between each guest/tenant that you have. The plus to doing short-term is that you get to charge a premium rate that is higher than you typically would charge someone that is staying for an extended period of time.

For example:

The average rental rate across the United States as of today is $2,000.00.

The nightly rate if you were to divide this by 30 days in a month would equal to $66.66/ day.

However, for a nightly rate it can vary by the place, however, for most places that offer an entire home fully furnished you can expect to see a rate of at LEAST $200 / night.

This means that if you were to rent out your home short-term for ONLY 10 days out of the month at the rate of $200 you could achieve the same amount that you could expect for an entire month.

Short-term= $200(daily rate) X 10(days) $2,000.00.

On the low end of renting for $200/ day you can reach that same $2,000 mark and still have the potential of surpassing and having a higher income. The other positive to this is you also get your money in advance prior to the stay guaranteed, opposed to tenants that may potentially be late or not pay on time and leave you responsible for still paying the monthly expenses. You have several different options when it comes to doing short-term renting as far as the platforms that you can utilize, the marketing strategies you can approach, and the clientele that you will have.

When it comes to doing long-term rentals, you also get your money upfront at the start of each month or whatever date you decide to have rent be paid by your tenants, but as you have your tenants on these longer agreements you cannot predict if there will be something unforeseen. There can be something unforeseen from your tenant's regular income and they might not be able to produce the money that you are requiring them to pay. However, at the same time you can do things like add late fees and other alternative methods to ensure that you have quality reliable tenants that will be credible and pay on time.

Ultimately, it all boils down to whether or not you are willing to take higher risk or if you would like to be more conservative you have the other option. Sometimes it can be good to do short-term during certain times of the year such as holidays, summer, or winter vacation and other seasons can be slower. In cases like this you would have to decide whether or not you are profiting enough during the busy seasons to where it can cover and account for the slow seasons. You also can play around between the two and see which type of renting is more beneficial for you and works better. This can be in the form of trying out the short-term and if it does not pick up begin marketing to long-term tenants simultaneously.

When you are exploring the different types of terms and agreements that you are considering to mix and match you will find that you have a great variety of tenant request types. Some are looking for day-to-day, some may need a month or so, and others may need a year or more. This is when you need to take a self-assessment and consider internally what you are looking to have accomplished in whatever time frame you have, then based upon the tools and resources you have find what your market is in your area for similar property types. For example, if people are renting a 3 bedroom/ 2 bathroom house for $1800/m you should not expect to rent an apartment that is a 3/2 bathroom bedroom in the same zip code for $2200. However, factors that you also look at are how renovated is the property, the square footage of the space, the utilities and amenities that are included or available, or even parking. When it comes to looking into renting your space for a shorter term there typically is that premium charge for not having a longer obligation, and in that case you might be able to find that you can rent a similar property type to continue with the example of a 3b/2ba if no one is satisfying the demand for short term rentals in your area you might be able to charge that higher amount for a smaller space if you allow for people to have shorter rental agreements. The beauty of it all is that you can always look to charge that premium amount for a shorter rental agreement and test the waters, and if that is not working out in your favour you can always switch and list it for longer terms. That way your property can start producing income, while it is being listed as available for long term rentals. This will allow you to have the time to conduct your due diligence on your new potential tenants prior to their move in date and schedule their walk through of your space around the short-term tenants booking dates.

The photo above depicts one of the short-term rentals that I have and you can see the different furnishings and features that it has. Some of the expenses here are a mortgage, appliances, internet, cleaning in between guest, and cleaning of the pool at this unit. There are more requirements when renting out for short-term rentals given that this is similar to a hotel stay, opposed to someone that is long-term as in most cases they will provide their own utilities and furniture. Initially, this can be a lot of upfront costs before you are able to make any money and therefore this is a perfect example of when you are able to utilize credit with 0% interest payments to allow your self time to make money with no money out of pocket from credit. As you are able to rent out your property, you are able to pay off the different items your purchased. This will takeaway from your profit in the beginning, but as you pay off your credit cards you will begin to profit even more!

9

Network

At this point you have already purchased your property and it is either rented out with tenants or you are in the stage where you purchased the property and are renovating it for potential tenants to move in. you will need to have a good network and team full of people that can service and prep your property or repair it, so that you do not have to compensate your tenants. A good team should have a handyman and cleaners. You can be more elaborate and have a home warranty policy, furniture connect, appliance connect, property management team, and real estate agents. The handyman can come and do small and possibly some major repairs and can be on call to run in and repair or adjust small things without needing a huge deductible for small wear and tear that the tenants will have during their stay. This can save you a lot of headaches of running and scrambling around to repair major or minor issues, if you can have someone that is constantly on call and knows and understands your space. Regardless of whether you are doing something for short or long term you will need to have a team of cleaners that can come in between each stay to ensure that the next set of guests are able to feel welcomed and invited knowing that they are in a freshly sanitated space. Cleaners can come in and do a deep cleaning to prevent dust build up, making sure carpets are deep cleaned, and more! In terms of home warranty policies this can allow for you to have that safety net of knowing if there is a major issue with the newly purchased home that a small deductible that is at a fixed price can ensure that a licensed professional within your area can come out to your home assess and repair any major fault whether it be something along the lines of a small plumbing leak in the kitchen or even on the worse case side such as a major electrical outage in half of your home. This is just a couple of examples; however, they can cover you in scenarios big and small and prevent you from having to come out of pocket from any major costs last minute. Home warranty is something that would cover costs that are not typically covered by your home insurance policy and is just another precaution you can have in place to allow yourself to be covered from any unexpected mishaps that can jeopardize your growing business. Finally, realtors can always update you with deals, word of mouth for vacancies you have, and in some cases be a connection for you to have with handymen, new deals, potential renters, home warranty recommendations, and more depending on their experience level and time in the field.

10

Knowing your demographic and market areas

An important factor to consider with the home you are renting is whether the area is ideally good for short-term renting or long-term renting. For example, good short-term rentals locations might be near places such as airports, amusement parks, etc. While good long-term rental locations might be near army bases, universities, or suburban areas where people can raise a family. This comes with the homework assignment of doing research and finding what amenities and community places that would attract your tenants, which is also key for marketing your property when you are ready to receive tenants. Looking up things like how far grocery stores are, places for public transportation, fun activities, educational places, or places for employment. This is a homework assignment you will have to do in order to find out if your property will be used for short or long term. Depending on what strategy you are aiming for will decipher whether or not you can look into a property in that particular area. Another good resource to utilize is your realtor or going out into the field and driving around to explore the area. Exploring the area is something that I would suggest everyone to do during the day time and the night time to in order you can see what type of people are in your area and how they are conducting themselves to see if this is an area where people are going to feel safe, if they can be entertained, and if they might like the area and why. This will tell you the different things you can utilize as a marketing tool when listing your property.

FROM ARMY TO MULTI MILLIONS IN REAL ESTATE | 39

(Airports are always a prime location for short-term rentals due to the high frequency of travelers coming in-and-out!)

Another aspect that comes along with knowing your demographic market is the homework assignment of knowing the laws and regulations that are in place in the different areas you are setting up your assets. Such as what permits are required when doing renovations or construction, this can come from calling the city or the county office your property is in and asking the need to know questions like, " Do I need to permits to do..." or "Am I allowed to build or do..." because if you are doing something that is not allowed by your county this can have many repercussions. Some of the repercussions you might be subject to are fines, court appearances, and things of that nature. The other homework assignment that follows is knowing the laws that are in favor of the tenants and in favor of the property owners. You have to have the knowledge of the procedures on how to evict tenants in the case of you finding tenants that are not in compliance with your rules and ensure that you are also in compliance at all times, and this will avoid you being subject to fines or penalties. Legally, there are somethings that you have to abide by when renting out a home long term to ensure that the home is sustainable, and this is also true whether your tenants pay or not. At times it will be situations where things are broken and not up to code for the county or state to the point of calling the home livable and you will be required to pay money and correct the situation, regardless of whether or not the tenants are paying or if they are the cause of the issue. There are somethings that might break or be altered from the way it was constructed and the owner will not be obligated to fix the issue and it will be the tenants responsibility. Things that are minor in most cases will fall on the tenant's responsibility and larger things will typically fall on responsibility of the home owner. The best case for this is to stay doing your homework and due diligence in staying knowledgeable of what the current laws are as it is subject to change at any time with a n update or change from the county.

11

Long-term VS Short term cash-returns

Now there are different agreements that you can make with your tenants or renters as far as the who, what, when, and whys. First, let us discuss the more traditional method which is long-term tenants. Long-term tenants are typically 6 months to a year on average. Sometimes it can be longer than a year, and in some cases a family might move into your home and not want to move out. There are different methods that owners will have set in place to protect theirself from tenants that also in a way keep the tenants from moving out and will make that tenant that was initially looking for a year-long contract, turn into multiple years or a lifetime. Sometimes a tenant simply cannot afford to move everything they have and pick up and go to another home. For the property owner, so long as your numbers made sense at the closing table you should be eager to have the tenants that will want to stay and rent for a lifetime because this simply makes your job that much easier! Now you get to have someone takeover all of your expenses and build equity in your property. As mentioned before your property will gain equity overtime with the more you pay off and as the supply and demand curve continuously shifts as it always does. The longer you have a tenant in your property and the less you have to come out of pocket to pay your own mortgage the better. You should want to never have to come out of pocket to cover your own mortgage, because this means that your tenants are literally making your equity grow for you and depending on the timeframe of your mortgage you may be done anywhere from 15-30 years depending on whether or not you refinance. You would want to refinance to alter and shift your Debt-to-income ratio (DTI), which is very important with the loan process as you intend to build your real estate portfolio. However, this is all depending on the way you calculated your numbers when you were doing your homework on potential rental amounts. If your numbers are already meeting your expectations, you may not need to look to refinance as this will only extend the years till your property is completely paid off. However, this is a case-by-case basis on if it is beneficial to refinance or not.

Now, when it comes to short-term renting this is a lot riskier! However, with the greater risk of doing this it can tend to have a far higher reward. Going based off of the median rental amount across the country of about $2,000 USD anywhere you are renting I have an example I would like to propose to you. Look at a place that goes for about $2,000 per month and if you were to take that same place and rent it for about $200 per day that would be far more profitable for you. Taking a place and renting it for short term there is always an upcharge or premium charge, just as in any hotel that you stay in you will see the same exact thing. The reason why all property owners do not do this is because it can propose far greater risk and run the potential threat of the owner having to come out of pocket to pay and cover a mortgage expense if they are not able to reach the required amount of tenants renting per month. The most popular form of short-term renting has been on Airbnb as of recent times. There are some other ways of renting that are short term that can also be very profitable that will be discussed more in my courses online in further detail. The short term rental game has many different ways of approaching it and it boils down to doing a little bit more homework on how you approach it and set it up, but upon proper research and initial set-up it can reach the point of being automated where you are able to seek great profits with little to no effort similar to long-term renting, but it depends on far more factors and each and every factors all come with the "what if" variable.... Personally, I find that it can be very profitable doing both options of long and short simultaneously in order to build and grow your empire, but it takes a little bit of timing just as all of real estate can essentially boil down to be.

12

Where do tenants come from?

You have done the research and the homework of running numbers on how to find the right property, you have made sure you can afford it even if you are not able to have it occupied by tenants, and you have your property in liveable conditions, and you are ready for tenants! You find yourself asking where the tenants come from and when do they start coming, or even when is the next one coming along, and this is another one of those risks. However, you can end up in some cases finding tenants immediately and in other cases it may not be as favourable. My first 4 homes that I purchased I had tenants immediately, literally faster than I could close I already had agreements for tenants long-term, and with my 5th home I had been waiting for quite an ample amount of time prior to finding any tenant that could rent my home. Which is all a part of the game and might mean that you need to change your strategy of long to short or vice versa. It might mean that you need to do a better job marketing a little differently and go a little harder with promotions.

This is one of the final steps until you can start seeing money actually coming in soon, however, you have to make sure that you do a great deal of due diligence given that you want to ensure that you find quality tenants that can afford your required rates and sustain making payments. It can be a tragic nightmare finding tenants that move in and do not pay on time, or even worse when they move in and do not pay rent at all. You are still required to pay the bill, and this can result in placing you in a very hard situation because you are still always going to be required to pay the mortgage on time regardless of whether your tenants pay their rent. This comes from doing extensive homework such as background checks, criminal checks, and prior rental history.

13

REFI to free-up VA home loan

Now, you have a home that you purchased through your state benefits, you have another home that you purchased through the VA benefits, and you are receiving a good amount of cash flow, and ready for your next project these are your options! You can either buy a secondary vacation home (Conventional) with 5% down payment or you can refinance (REFI), which is transforming the loan type you have from VA home loan into a conventional loan. This will do a couple of things to your investment. One it will change the interest rate, which is something that you need to be very cognizant of and pay attention to as it may possibly increase your monthly payments or decrease your payments. Thus, this can be both beneficial and harmful depending on what your profit margins are for your property. If you purchased at a rate of 6%, and refinance when rates decrease to 4% you will increase your profit margin and free-up your VA home loan, and that will allow you to purchase another property again with no money down. Also, when it comes to refinancing your home you are able to either pay the refinancing fees upfront out of your pocket, or inquire about including them into your new loan. Meaning you can free up the entire loan and do so with no money out of your pocket. On the other hand, if you used your VA home loan at a 4% and are looking to refinance when rates are higher, you will be paying more on your monthly mortgage at the cost of freeing up your VA home loan benefits. This is something that would require homework and running the numbers to see what makes the most sense given that specific situation. Questions to think about are how it will affect your debt-to-income ratio (DTI), will it increase or decrease your home buying power.

14

What's not seen, or told in real estate?

Realtors

Real estate agents, commonly known as realtors, are professionals who help individuals buy, sell, or rent properties. While they are knowledgeable about the real estate industry, it is important to note that not all realtors are investors. Sometimes you will strike the dice and get lucky and come across some people that are here in your corner and would like your best interest because they love their job and simply would like to assist people reach their dreams of either financial freedom or the American dream of owning a home, however, this is not always the case. From my experience, I have not met a realtor that has told me "This is not a good investment property" they more commonly say something along the lines of "this house just needs a little bit of TLC" or something that still is geared toward you buying and them getting their commission. Once again, not to paint the picture of this being a constant factor for all realtors. There are some that will give you real advice and guidance, however, this is research to inform that you have to be on your toes and actively studying and conducting due diligence yourself because not everyone is going to be real and you will come across several people that are a yes-man.

According to a survey conducted by the National Association of Realtors (NAR), only 15% of realtors own investment properties. This is a small percentage compared to the number of realtors in the United States. The same survey also revealed that 72% of realtors have never invested in real estate. This suggests that the majority of realtors focus solely on helping their clients buy and sell properties, rather than investing in real estate themselves. Moreover, realtors who specialize in residential real estate tend to have less experience in real estate investing. According to an article by Forbes, most residential real estate agents are not investors because they do not have the necessary knowledge or resources to invest. They may not have access to the same investment opportunities as experienced investors, nor do they have the financial means to invest in properties themselves.

However, real estate agents are often required to adhere to ethical standards and regulations that may prevent them from investing in certain properties. For instance, the National Association of Realtors Code of Ethics requires realtors to disclose any personal interest in a property they are selling. This means that realtors who invest in properties they are selling may be seen as having a conflict of interest, which can damage their reputation and credibility.

Furthermore, being a successful investor requires a different set of skills than being a successful realtor. While realtors need to be knowledgeable about the real estate market and have strong communication and negotiation skills, investors need to have a deeper understanding of financial analysis, risk management, and property management. Therefore, being a realtor does not necessarily translate to being a successful investor.

In conclusion, while some realtors may be investors, the majority are not. According to the National Association of Realtors, only 15% of realtors own investment properties. Realtors who specialize in residential real estate tend to have less experience in real estate investing, and ethical standards and regulations may prevent them from investing in certain properties. Being a successful investor requires a different set of skills than being a successful realtor, and not all realtors possess these skills.

PMI/ DOWNPAYMENT

PMI is an insurance policy that lenders require borrowers to purchase when they are unable to make a down payment of at least 20% of the home purchase price. PMI premiums are typically added to the monthly mortgage payment and can range from 0.3% to 1.5% of the original loan amount. The cost of PMI varies depending on the size of the down payment, the loan amount, and the borrower's credit score.

Pros of PMI

Lower down payment requirement: One of the main advantages of PMI is that it allows borrowers to purchase a home with a lower down payment than the traditional 20%. This is beneficial for those who may not have enough savings to make a large down payment.

Access to homeownership: PMI can help make homeownership accessible to borrowers who may not have been able to afford it otherwise. This can be especially helpful for first-time homebuyers who are just starting out and do not have a lot of savings. (When buying a home and you are getting your approval from the bank, they are going to assess your Debt-To-Income Ratio (DTI) and as they are consolidating your monthly expenses if you can pay down a big amount you will be able to qualify on your purchase because the mortgage will drop in monthly cost. This lump payment can come from a friend or family member as a gift.

Tax-deductible: PMI premiums can be tax-deductible for borrowers who meet certain criteria. This can help offset the cost of the insurance and reduce the overall cost of homeownership. (Please consult with your CPA, and further discuss whether or not this is something that applies to your circumstances)

Cons of PMI

Additional cost: PMI adds an additional cost to the monthly mortgage payment, which can make homeownership more expensive. This can also increase the debt-to-income ratio, which can make it harder to qualify for other types of loans.

Limited benefit: PMI only benefits the lender and does not offer any protection to the borrower. In the event of a default, the lender is protected, but the borrower may still lose their home and their investment.

Difficult to cancel: Cancelling PMI can be difficult and time-consuming. Borrowers may have to wait until they have paid off a certain percentage of the loan or until the home has appreciated in value before they can cancel the insurance.

In conclusion, PMI is an insurance policy that lenders may require borrowers to purchase when they are unable to make a down payment of at least 20%. The pros of PMI include a lower down payment requirement, access to homeownership, and tax-deductibility. The cons of PMI include additional cost, limited benefit, and difficulty in cancelling. Before purchasing a home, borrowers should consider the pros and cons of PMI and weigh their options carefully. Whether or not you should do this in my experience is a case-by-case basis depending on your particular strategy and what you would like to see long term. For example, if your goal is to get the home that you believe to be a good property for cheap then fix it and flip it later this may not be a strategy that interests you. If you are looking to keep this property long term as a rental for either short or long-term it may not be of interest, you. It all takes consideration and running your numbers and doing your homework at the end of the day.

BUYING DOWN INTEREST RATES

One of the most significant factors affecting homeownership is interest rates on mortgages. A high-interest rate can significantly increase the total cost of homeownership. However, many homeowners can lower their mortgage interest rates by "buying down" their interest rates. This section explores different ways to buy down interest rates for a home in order to lower your monthly payments on your new home.

Points

Points are an upfront fee paid to the lender at the time of closing to lower the interest rate on a mortgage loan. One point is equal to 1% of the total loan amount. For instance, if the loan amount is $200,000, one point would cost $2,000. The borrower can choose to pay points to lower the interest rate on the mortgage, with each point typically lowering the rate by 0.25%. However, paying points only makes sense if the homeowner plans to stay in the house long enough to recoup the cost of the points through lower monthly mortgage payments.

Refinance

Another way to buy down interest rates is to refinance the existing mortgage. Refinancing involves obtaining a new mortgage loan to replace the existing mortgage. The new loan comes with a lower interest rate, resulting in lower monthly mortgage payments. Homeowners can refinance their mortgage loans through their existing lenders or other lenders in the market. However, homeowners should only refinance if the savings in interest payments outweigh the costs of refinancing. Most banking institutions will have some sort of tracker available that will make this something easy to view in terms of calculating your homework, and in terms of refinancing this should be something that is viewable in the loan disclosures you are signing. Yet, you still have to view and assess your personal goals and consider your debt-to-income (DTI) and if the payments of your monthly mortgage will be lower and this is more important to you given your current circumstances this might be something you want to consider, however, be informed and know that you will overall be paying more in the long run if the interest charges from your refinancing outweighs the current loan.

Adjustable-Rate Mortgages

Adjustable-rate mortgages (ARMs) are mortgage loans with interest rates that can fluctuate based on market conditions. ARMs generally offer lower interest rates than fixed-rate mortgages (FRMs) in the initial years of the loan. However, the interest rate can increase after the initial period, leading to higher monthly mortgage payments. Homeowners can "buy down" the interest rate on ARMs by paying discount points, which lower the interest rate in exchange for an upfront fee. This is something that typically I would recommend avoiding for the simple fact that I would like to know that all of my monthly expenses are solidified and will not change. As I plan to build my portfolio it gives peace of mind knowing that now and indefinitely moving forward in the years to come what my minimum payments will be unless I do something that changes those numbers through some form of refinancing.

Government Programs

Government programs, such as the Federal Housing Administration (FHA) and the Department of Veterans Affairs (VA), offer mortgage loans with lower interest rates to qualified borrowers. FHA loans require a lower down payment than traditional mortgage loans, making it easier for first-time homebuyers to purchase homes. Similarly, VA loans offer zero down payment and lower interest rates to military service members and veterans. However, as previously stated earlier in this book there are tons of programs available through the government in each and every state in the country. With that being said VA is no money down, however you are still paying closing costs. FHA is typically 3.5% of the home sale price down as well as closing costs. As of now, there are several programs available that allow for you to pay no down payment and in some cases have assistance with closing costs or no closing costs as well. With that being said, I would HIGHLY RECOMMEND doing your research and using one of these programs prior to using your VA home loan. This is for the simple fact that these government programs are in most cases for your FIRST home loan, and the VA can be utilized regardless of how many homes you own as long as it is for your primary home. This is probably one of the biggest takeaways from this book that I can offer you to build your portfolio. The goal that you can initially meet is building your portfolio using as little money as possible and through the means of as many benefits or government assistance as possible. There are many variables that can come into play after, however, using this blueprint and depending on the price points of the homes that you are seeking this can allow you to get several pieces of real property with little to no money being used based on how you go about negotiating closing costs, government assistance, and state benefits.

To summarize, buying down interest rates is an excellent way for homeowners to save money on their mortgage payments. Points, refinancing, ARMs, and government programs are all effective ways to lower interest rates on mortgage loans. Homeowners should weigh the costs and benefits of each option before deciding which one to pursue. While buying down interest rates can help homeowners save money, it is essential to understand the risks and potential downsides of each approach.

PROPERTY MANAGEMENT

In the world of real estate, there are many subcategories and opportunities that have been around for decades and new ones that are also presenting their selves. When renting a property at residentially there are many factors that must be taken into account given that states differentiate in the laws of which they have for those that have diversified their portfolio, and to make matters even more difficult the government enforced laws can differentiate in the same city from county to county. As someone who has not always had a goal in making real estate that primary income the hassles that can present their selves as a property owner. The money can come in and be good, but it's the different unforeseen headaches that can cause issues later down the line legally that we can plan for and never want to occur. A saviour to this issue can be a property management company! A property management company should be a subject matter expert for you as a homeowner and investor.

They should be knowledgeable of the different laws and regulations that are active and changing state-wide and across the county.

The property management company is a part of your team and your employee, which means they are also a tax write off for you (please consult with your CPA). You should have clear and concise communication with your team at all times on what you are looking for from your property in order to meet and maintain being on track with your goals, and they should be able to give you a full and honest response on whether or not that is possible with a plan. Different companies operate differently and therefore you have more homework when it comes to finding people that understand your vision and are willing to meet your criteria in order to work effectively with you. Most companies will have a procedure of which they typically operate and be able to meet your needs and demands, so that you are able to see long-term success. They should have a team of people who they can call on to have reliable and trustworthy handymen come and service your home, a procedure of screening trustworthy tenants that will pay on time, an eviction process that includes them being able to represent you in court in case of your absence, and thus leaving you able to focus on what is in front of your life outside of real estate while still collecting the fruits of your investments..

CONTRACTORS

Contractors are someone that may or may not be required for you in your journey, however, in the case a job or service that is needed is out of the scope and capabilities of your handyman this is someone that you want to have in your pocket as well. When it comes to a contractor you can have one that is specific to the trade that you are looking to have worked on such as plumbing, electrical, or floor installation. A contractor that is able to tackle of all of your home needs is referred to as a general contractor, and they typically oversee a project similar to a project manager/site manager. They have a team of people that work underneath them that are working under their supervision to complete your project. This has both its PRO's and CON's given that they are not doing the work and have to pay more people for having their network of employees you the owner are left paying a form of convenience fee. They are going to charge you a higher amount, so that they can pay their employees and their self at the same time which is the downside. The positive side to this is that you save yourself the headache of trying out new contractors that specialize in each respective field and having one person to hold accountable in the case of anything going wrong.

    This was an opportunity I seen in a property for what is called an Additional Dwelling Unit (ADU). The home I was purchasing had a 4-car garage and was over 2,000 sqft, so I took this as an opportunity to expand and maximize profits at one property. Doing this could allow for me to receive two incomes from one property or allow for me to stay in one unit and rent the other. This is another form of house hacking and scaling properties. This is something that you would need to check with your county and see if it is something that is allowed to be done, to avoid citations and having to tear it down you will need to get everything done with permits.

DO NOT GET SCAMMED

There are some people that are not as honest in the world, and I would like to inform you about how to verify if the people that you are working with are legitimate. Every individual that claims to be a realtor or loan officer will have an NMLS number that is almost like an employee identification to show whether they are actually who they say they are and qualified to work with you. If they are not able to provide you with the number, it would be highly advised NOT to work with them. Given the fact that the loan process requires your sensitive information you should not render the information they are going to request from you lightly because it can result in a form of fraudulent activity or impersonation of your identity.

The National Mortgage Licensing System and Registry (NMLS) was established by the federal government to provide a single source of information and licensing for mortgage professionals in the United States. The NMLS allows consumers to verify the licensing status of mortgage professionals such as realtors and loan officers, ensuring that they are qualified and authorized to work in their respective fields. Each realtor or loan officer has to be licensed in the states individually, ensure that you follow these steps below so you can rest assured knowing that they are licensed in the state you are looking to purchase in.

Here are the steps to identify a realtor or loan officer by their NMLS:

Know the NMLS identification number format: An NMLS identification number is a unique 7-digit number assigned to each individual mortgage professional registered in the NMLS system. The format of an NMLS ID number is 1 letter followed by 6 digits (e.g., M123456). The first letter identifies the type of license, for example, "M" for mortgage loan originator or "R" for real estate broker.

Obtain the NMLS identification number: The NMLS identification number can be found on the mortgage professional's business card, website, or marketing materials. It is also required by law to be displayed on any loan application or other mortgage-related documents provided to the borrower.

Check the NMLS Consumer Access website: The NMLS Consumer Access website (www.nmlsconsumeraccess.org) is a free online database that provides information about licensed mortgage professionals, including real estate brokers and loan officers. To verify the NMLS identification number, enter the professional's name and state of residence or business, and their NMLS ID number.

Review the mortgage professional's record: Once you enter the NMLS ID number on the Consumer Access website, you will be able to review the professional's record. This will include their full name, business name, contact information, license status, and any disciplinary actions or sanctions that may have been taken against them.

Confirm the license status: The NMLS Consumer Access website will indicate whether the professional's license is currently active or inactive. If the license is inactive, it means the professional is not authorized to conduct mortgage-related business. If the license is active, it means they are authorized and qualified to work in their field.

Look for additional credentials: In addition to an NMLS ID number, real estate brokers and loan officers may also have other professional designations or certifications, such as a Certified Mortgage Planning Specialist (CMPS) or Accredited Mortgage Professional (AMP). These credentials can indicate that the professional has additional training and expertise in their field.

In conclusion, verifying a realtor or loan officer's NMLS identification number is an important step in ensuring that they are authorized and qualified to work in their respective fields. By following these steps, consumers can have confidence that they are working with a licensed professional who is committed to providing ethical and professional mortgage services.

15

Closing

Following these steps shall help you acquire a few pieces of investment property as well as a primary residence. Maintaining the properties can produce not only a monthly cashflow, however, it also can grow equity. My personal preference with different methods is to buy-and-hold opposed to the popular "Fix and Flip" strategies that have grown to be more common in the more recent years. However, I do find and believe that the BRRRR can be a very good method from what I have seen but is not something I have fully invested my resources or focus on at this time. My reasoning behind staying away from the Fix and Flip strategy, is that the median rental amount across the United States is around $2,000 to $2,500. To make more logic in this to myself I asked myself how much money I would want to live comfortably to retire. The number I gave myself is $10,000 each month passively, with that number in mind I would need to have at least four-five rentals to achieve that goal. However, repeating this process will assist you in achieving your goals. Whether you have the goal of being a designer, building cars, or working in the film industry having passive income through real estate will give you the financial stability needed to pursue your dreams and not have to worry about struggling. The other benefits that come along with a real estate portfolio is that you can also borrow against your home if you ever have financial issues come about, if you would like to pass down generational wealth to your family, or even have the opportunity to become your own employer and work on your own timing.

Also, with this field of work there can be some downsides. You can run into tenants that do not pay, you can find a place that may have tenants that are squatting, or you might run into issues that need major repairs. However, there are several remedies that will assist with that. There is home-owners insurance, there is a home warranty, you can have a team of handymen or contractors, or even begin Do it yourself (DIY) projects and fix the property yourself. There are downsides and several scenarios that you can run into as speed bumps, but there are fixes that you can have to make it work smoothly. The best analogy I can give is working with a car, which is another major investment that you can make, and you would also have insurance with this or a warranty on the different high-end features that can tend to be costly such as the tires or different customizable features on it. The name of the game is acquire and then protect your assets, take care of them and they will be able to take care of you.

16

Resources

Home searching sites
Zillow
Realtor.com
Redfin

Helpful Sources
Bankrate (best for particular type of loans)
Home buying programs by state
Mortgage calculators
Interest Saving Calculator
CoreLogic [Track home equity reports (H.E.R.)]
www.nmlsconsumeraccess.org

17

References

Blue Star Families. (2019)

Bureau of Labor Statistics. (2021). Employment Situation of Veterans — 2020. Retrieved from https://www.bls.gov/news.release/pdf/vet.pdf

Cook, L. (n.d.). Mortgage > VA Loans. Money.com. https://money.com/how-to-refinance-a-va-loan/

Department of Veterans Affairs. (2021). Interest Rate Reduction Refinance Loan. Retrieved from https://www.va.gov/housing-assistance/home-loans/irrrl/

Federal Reserve Bank of St. Louis. (n.d.). What are points? Retrieved from https://www.stlouisfed.org/financial-institution-supervision/credit-risk-management/what-are-points

Investopedia. (2022). Adjustable-rate mortgage - ARM. Retrieved from https://www.investopedia.com/terms/a/arm.asp

Investopedia. (2022). Interest Rate Reduction Refinance Loan (IRRRL). Retrieved from https://www.investopedia.com/terms/i/irrrl.asp

Mcmillin, D. (2022, November 28). BankRate. Bankrate. https://www.bankrate.com/home-equity/homeowner-equity-data-and-statistics/

(n.d.). MortgageCalculator. Mortgage Calculator. https://www.mortgagecalculator.org/

National Association of Realtors. (2020). Social benefits of homeownership and stable housing. Retrieved from https://www.nar.realtor/research-and-statistics/research-reports/social-benefits-of-homeownership-and-stable-housing

(n.d.). Realtor.Com. Realtor.com. https://www.realtor.com/?cid=sem_425822242_1236950839353931_:G:s&s_kwcid=AL!15120!3!!e!!o!!realtor&gclid=86dfa5abd2b210a8144bc6175d24f093&gclsrc=3p.ds&msclkid=86dfa5abd2b210a8144bc6175d24f093

(n.d.). Redfin. Redfin. https://www.redfin.com/

Tax Policy Center. (2020). Tax deductions and homeownership. Retrieved from https://www.taxpolicycenter.org/briefingbook/what-tax-deduction-homeownership

(n.d.). The Mortgage Reports. First Time Home Buyer Program in All 50 States. https://themortgagereports.com/64872/first-time-home-buyer-programs-50-states

U.S. Department of Housing and Urban Development. (n.d.). Refinancing your home. Retrieved from https://www.hud.gov/topics/refinancing

U.S. Department of Veterans Affairs. (n.d.). VA loans. Retrieved from https://www.benefits.va.gov/homeloans/index.asp

(n.d.). Zillow. Zillow. https://www.zillow.com/

(n.d.). 2023CoreLogic. CoreLogic. https://www.corelogic.com/category/intelligence/reports/homeowner-equity/

About the Author

Born and raised in South Central Los Angeles, California Clavacia Love Smith grew up the eldest of four children in a single-family household. Attending Crenshaw High School and playing football all four years he was able to obtain two out-of-state scholarship offers to play defensive-end. The seventeen year-old high school senior had to make adult decisions as the senior year of high-school was approaching an end and decided to stay local to his hometown to allow for him to be closer to his family in the case he needed to support his younger siblings as family has always been very important to him. Attending California State University of Northridge he was still within a driveable distance to home. He then dropped out of college after two semesters in order to enlist in the Army Reserve to assist with college tuition fees. Initially enlisting as a 91B (Light Wheeled Vehicle Mechanic) for a chemical unit in southern California, he found that he wanted to pursue a different route within the military. He found himself enrolling in R.O.T.C. at the

University of California Los Angeles where he was on the path to becoming a junior officer in the Army.

After several years of him serving he became eligible for the VA home loan where he was able to purchase his first home in Atlanta, Georgia. He began to study and conduct research in the field of Real Estate following the footsteps of his great grandmother. Mr. Smith found that he was able to conduct a "formula" for receiving passive income from his real estate and then was able to quickly grow and expand his portfolio within a very abrupt timeframe. He found that he was able to purchase five rentals within a window just over a year. By this time he had found a deep love and passion for the industry and began to find himself mentoring and coaching family and friends on the subject.

Currently, he is expanding his portfolio through other means of obtaining real estate in ways such as property auctions, new construction, and even real estate stocks. When asked to leave a quote on the subject he quoted his great grandmother Gwendolyn saying, "They are not making any more Earth, so buy up as much as you can" one thing that is for certain is that this is not something that he took lightly as his resume shows that once he started, there was no sign of stopping.

Connect with the author for more one on one training, updates, and insights here!

Social media

Email: Clavacialove@gmail.com

One Last Thing!

If you enjoyed the book, please take a moment of your time to leave a review with your thoughts. I encourage you to utilize the contents within this book to your advantage as a resource as you are starting your journey and building your portfolio. I look forward to publishing more work as well as creating courses that are more hands-on and personal to better assist, inform, and teach!

Clavacialove@gmail.com
Thanks again for your support!

www.ingramcontent.com/pod-product-compliance
Lightning Source LLC
Chambersburg PA
CBHW041428140226
39719CB00035B/6